# WOMEN
# ACROSS
# BORDERS

## with a mission

Dr. Sonia Noel
Copyright © 2018 Sonia Noel
All rights reserved.
ISBN-13: 978-1987695007
ISBN-10: 1987695003

Creative Direction:  Richard Young

Editor: Desiree De Florimonte

Book layout and design: Shiv Dindyal

# FOREWORD
## DR. LINDA WALLACE

Now is an era when women can just as easily have a sisterhood in another nation as in their own hometown. With the advancement of technology we are afforded the opportunity to be part of a global community of incredible, talented, powerful women who are fulfilling their mission and callings in their sphere of influence. Sonia Noel is one of those women. In a WhatsApp chat, we shared for hours our mutual passion for serving and empowering women, globally. Sonisia attended an event held in Los Angeles where women from all spheres where gathered to learn about values and principles that help women to live by a code. In a subsequent conversation with Sonia, she shared with me the many projects and initiatives she was leading in her native country, Guyana. I said to her with all the acts of kindness, civic and business activities you are engaged in, it sounds like you are leading a "Love Revolution."

Those words would actually result in the launch of a movement with an amazing event hosted by Sonia, in Guyana, where hundreds of political, business, civic and religious leaders attended. I was honoured to be the keynote speaker, all from a phone call!

This is the power of Women Across Borders. When you engage with other women of different ethnic backgrounds and mutually share your stories, amazing opportunities can happen. Purpose can be discovered, collaborations can result in the lives of entire nations being impacted. The Women Across Borders Movement, is a project that allows women to tell their stories, victories and processes of transformation while being their authentic, transparent selves. They are then able to release other women to experience freedom. I highly recommend that you get to your favourite place, grab that cup of coffee, tea or glass of wine and go on by following these women, across borders. You will get a glimpse into their lives, callings and mission as each one pursues their passion, identity and destiny!

# DEDICATION

I dedicate this book to all the organizations, groups and movements who are transforming the lives of women and girls around the world.

# ACKNOWLEDGEMENT

Launching two Anthologies within a week is no easy task but for those who know me are not surprise with the way I challenge myself .My passion for people drives me but my faith in God knowing the victory is ours and the battle is his. WOMEN ACROSS BORDERS is a perfect gift for International Women's Day.

These eight riveting stories could not have been possible without some phenomenal women I met over the year. The number 8 has special meanings and some are: 8 balances the material and immaterial worlds; eight is also associated with the beginning of a new era or that of a new order; it represents Infinity and everything good in the universe which is infinite, such as infinite love, infinite supply, infinite energy etc. Number 8 resonates with the influences and vibrations of authority and personal power, self-confidence, executive ability, confidence, inner-strength, material freedom and success. I love, appreciate and I'm inspired by these women. You sisters did not hesitate to join me on this other crucial leg of my journey even without knowing all of the details. Christine Neblett, you are a go getter and display so much strength even when things seem chaotic around you. Isabelle D Ngcobo, you remind me of the kids in schools you miss when they don't attend but still want them to stay lol Can't help but love you my sister. Chan Tale Flood, you are such a delicate soul that scares me sometimes but your love for God reassures me that you will be fine. Linda Felix Johnson, you are a tower of strength that is contagious. Ediclia Bastardo, you have a big heart and your love for people encourage me to love even more. Bethany Hanna, you are such a sweetheart with those pretty blue eyes that sometimes reflect pain than I confident is turning into purpose. Essenese Sambury, it is truly a miracle you are still with us and God spared you to take you on a mission. Linda Wallace, the words in your foreword touched me to the core and I must thank for all the spiritual support you have given.

You are contributing significantly to humanity. Compton, your talent is beyond what you imagine it to be and you captured the cover in a magnificent artistic expression. When I envisioned the cover, I thought about our lives as individuals and how we started as a blank canvas but our actions determined the various paintings that shaped our lives. We decide the color, paint and size of paintbrush to use through this journey called life. Richard and Shiv, your creative direction is invaluable. Ediclia, you made these words possible from English to Spanish and Alize to French. Denielle, you went beyond the call for this project and I love and appreciate you. To Kidd Marketing for your support and advice.

To all the people who contributed in any way to make this project a reality as we continue this mission to make a difference in the lives of people across borders.

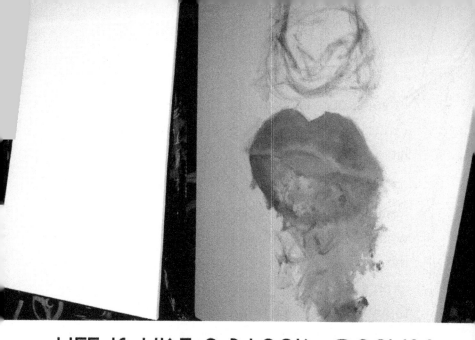

# LIFE IS LIKE A BLANK CANVAS
## Artist Compton Babb

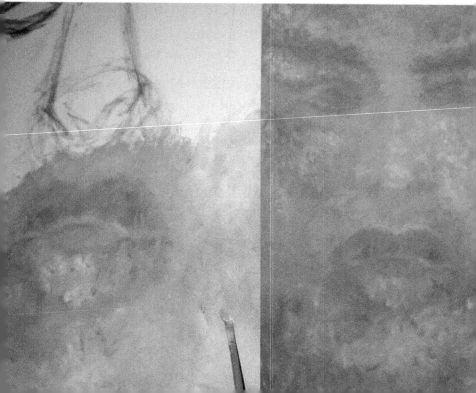

# TABLE OF CONTENTS

# CHAPTER 1
## *Live Your Life With Intention And See It Roar*

Bethany Love.

My name is Bethany Love and I am here to connect with you and help you find your voice, courage and story within mine. I am here to inspire you! When reading, feel into the parts that resonates with you and where you may be struggling and how it may help you. One book, 1 sentence or 1 word can majorly affect your life. Know that you are beautiful, unique and a true miracle! We all hold a unique energy signature which plays its part in this world and universe and there will never be another repeated. Take ownership of you and your uniqueness; stand tall and brightly... the world needs you and you need you!!

Here goes... writing this is as healing for me as it may be an inspiration for you to make a move in your life. Not too long ago, I was in a state of despair in my life... Not every day, but overall as I did not know how to get out of where I WAS... and I wondered if it would ever happen.... About 3 ½ years ago I ended a very hard chapter of my life..... 13 years of my life went by that I will never get back. Lost in a state of fear, despair, and cloudiness my life was spinning out of control at a faster rate than ever before in the year of 2014. I knew there had to be a way out, but I did not know how it would happen or when. I believed if I didn't I surely would not have made it... literally. I cried out to God. It was the beginning of August 2014 when I actually screamed at HIM and said, "Do something, because I can't." I was sitting in a dressing room where I worked with an eye swollen shut and the other one was blurry too. I could hardly see, and I was angry, angry at life and angry that no matter how hard I seemed to pray that things remained the same. I wanted my daughter to have a life that was safe and secure, where she did not have to be scared but where she saw love practiced every day and not yelling, screaming and violence. She deserved more and I deserved more. The answer came about 10 days later...

To catch you up, I was in very toxic and abusive relationship on and off for 13 years with the father of my child. Inside this relationship I experienced verbal, mental, emotional, physical, spiritual, financial and sexual abuse. We started dating when I was

17, and we started off rocky. The warning signs were there or what you call "RED FLAGS," however I did not know this language until I took a domestic violence class years later. I had grown up with so much love and didn't even realize this world existed. I was in 'la la land.'

I am going to take you through a 3 or 4 experiences that were truly some of the hardest times in my life and walk you through how I overcame and eventually came out.

In 2006, my daughter was about 6 months old. I got into an argument with my ex about going shopping with him for our daughter. I had not been since she was born and was so upset that he was going shopping with another woman for our daughter. How could he when we had never done this together? I LOST IT! I was so very angry. Looking back my feelings were valid, however based on an overview of what came from this; it was minimal.

Now, things were not good emotionally, spiritually or physically at the time. It was hard being a new mother, working every day, not getting much sleep or time with my baby daughter nor love from him. I was on edge. From that day on, my ex and I split for about 5 months. We had a bad physical altercation. I jumped in front of his car as he was pulling out of our driveway leaving with our daughter and the other woman he was speaking to at the time. He stopped and I ran around to pull our daughter out of her seat, but he jumped out of the driver's seat and dragged me into the master bedroom by my hair. He tore about half of my hair out. From there he was physically, verbally and emotionally abusive. I left and starting walking to my parent's home which was about 6 or 7 miles from where we lived. I was picked up by the police, who came driving by because he had called them to check on me. The reason why it was so painful was that I was away from my daughter for so long. Her father wouldn't let me see her unless I came over to his place and I refused as I knew if I went back that the cycle would continue. I ended up going back since I couldn't take being away from her any longer. During this time I grew stronger, and learned how to really rely on God. I got rejuvenated with sleep, positive people and love and most of all time with myself to really pray and meditate. Every time I left, as I left multiple times, I grew stronger, and I grew a little wiser and I knew one day things would change. I journaled a lot, and took a lot of walks.

Another really hard time for me was in 2009 with my daughter. I lost in the custody battle with my ex. It was devastating and I didn't know how this could happen when I told the truth. I was angry, sad, in despair and didn't understand why this was happening when I was doing the right thing for our daughter. What led up to this was another time when I thought something really bad physically was going to happen to me, so I bolted out the garage door of our house and ran across the street barefoot. Our daughter was currently with my family so it worked in my favour and I left the state with her so he could not come get her from me, therefore continuing the cycle. I left for 6 months and got an attorney to try and solve this with the courts involvement. The sad thing is I never called the police when he hit me and physically harmed me, so there was no record and the courts ruled in his favour as I had left and not let him see her until we had supervised visits set up. When I lost, I realized that I had no idea how I was going to move on in life with someone else basically raising my daughter. Being able to raise my daughter and spend time with her was basically all I wanted to do. I went back to him and his wife at the time … weird situation but I wanted to be with my daughter.

What I learned from this situation is that I had to have patience. One day things would work out. I stayed hopeful even in my pain. I knew that it couldn't always stay this way even though it seemed like it would. I stood up for myself and I did what was right and lost, however I lost the fight not the battle. Have you ever been in a situation where you wondered will things ever change? Why when I am doing the right thing, does it seem to get worse? Or are you there now? Take peace in knowing that things will get better and you can change them when you stand in your power.

Another time that was so painful was in 2014, when my ex held 2 knives to my chest and told me if I didn't tell him the truth he would stab me 67 times. This was very scary, yes, it lasted for 3 hours and I remember thinking if I make it out of here … it will be a miracle and I will change my life. I also thought I can't die because my daughter cannot live with him and people not know what he is capable of. I have to survive and somehow create a life for her and get her out. What was the saddest thing I have ever done was to leave my daughter with him… I escaped but I knew I couldn't get her out and make it. I knew if I tried and he caught me I would not be here. Her only hope of getting out was me getting to safety and getting on my feet. So I left her. But that's not the hard part, the hard part was I knew I could not call the police on him, or that's how I felt. We were doing drugs at the time and he would pin it on me and I would lose her to him forever. He also, threatened the lives of all of my family if I ever left again and said that he would not kill me but make me wish I was dead.

I knew I would have to be decisive and somehow get my daughter out but I felt I had to do it on my own. Well, I went back because I couldn't bear not being with my child and knowing if she was okay. He would not let me see her except one time at my sister's house then later he said I had to come to his place. I went back with the mindset of getting my daughter out whatever it took, even if I died or went to prison. I wanted her to have a life.

Coming back to August 2014. Things had gotten really bad and I screamed at God to do something and to get my daughter and me out. I need help and I didn't know what to do.

On the night of August 13th- my life would change forever. My ex, physically assaulted another woman and then dropped her off at the hospital. I was at work, so I had no knowledge any of this happened. We stayed in a motel that night because our gas had been turned off due to non-payment. We had no hot water and we wanted to take a hot shower. Our bill was $1,300. We had the money to pay the night before but he gave it to someone else for a business deal he was doing. Long story- short, we were walking out of Motel 6 as we did not have much money at the time, even though we were leasing a 5,500 square foot house and driving a Masarati. I remember my ex saying, "I feel like I have not slept in 10 years." We awoke and were walking towards our car. Suddenly, as we got in I saw someone was running towards us. Yes, it was SWAT surrounding our car and blocking us in. My ex said, "Babe I didn't do anything." That was the last time I saw or spoke to him, August 14, 2014. I still remember thanking God for this intervention from the law. I knew my prayers had been answered! It was in a very corrective way, but it provided space, time and most importantly my daughter's safety.

The hardest thing for me was knowing that because of my choices and being with someone who was not healthy, my daughter suffered extreme abuse. Knowing that she was abused by her father, I felt 100 percent responsible because I am her mother and it is my job to protect her. I was unable to truly love myself for a while but found my way back with family, God, prayer, mediation, reading, walking and spending time with quality people.

I want everyone to know that you can always get back up on your feet wherever you are. Never stop believing in yourself or your worth! Don't let your past dictate your future. Let it be a stepping stone for your future. I am a better person today with all of my painful experiences. The only thing I truly wish I could take back is the abuse to my daughter. However, I know with the right love, structure and support my daughter will heal overtime and she will do amazing things in this world. Don't hate yourself, don't judge yourself, find yourself, find your voice, speak up and speak out. I believe in you and you are loved.

My daughter and I now live together, and I am working on a couple of businesses. We are learning how to live together again and how to understand each other. I have the greatest gift I could ever ask for: my life and my daughter's life! I challenge you today to look at your life and to be grateful you are alive! Now take this life and create! God gave you everything you need. You are magnificent without doing anything, just being you. Remember who you are and dive deep within your soul for the answers are there.

# CHAPTER 2

# *I Found My Salvation In Christ*

Chan Tale Flood.

Life is not always easy and a lot of times unfair. I was never in search of perfection ... I was in search of being enough. Little did I know enough was the variable. Adequacy wasn't always measured by my standard but a lot by the ones I was depending on for the 'enough.'

I remember as a child I always had a vivid imagination of life. Looking back at it, I can almost say for sure that I created my own reality and that reality was mine ... no one else's, and it was exactly how I saw life at the moment.

My rights were right, and I didn't have a lot of wrongs. That worked out fine until I was about the age of eleven.

As a teenager I became rebellious, angry, verbally aggressive and lonely. At the time I didn't know it was loneliness. I skipped school just to hang out and that resulted in fights at home which changed the relationship between me and my sister. She distanced herself from me because she was embarrassed.

I remember that one night, my mother didn't want me to go out but I had already planned a night out with friends. I wore my clothes with my pyjamas over them. As soon as I knew everyone was asleep I slipped through the window just to get out the house. Things like that embarrassed my sister.

Although I always did well in school, I was never part of any group. I had my own thing and did my own thing, on my own.

I moved to Europe and became conscious of my emptiness, emotional disconnect and rollercoaster behaviour. By the time I was 17, I was working and started my independence at the age of 18.

The Big City

I moved from our small, almost village-like home to the big city. Working, going to college and dealing with disorders I didn't know I had wasn't the easiest part of life. After years of unconscious captivity and being all by myself, forced me to confront my anxiety … but I couldn't. I had all these new wells that needed exploiting so I forced my anxiety back in captivity by creating new worlds. Bigger and better than the ones from my childhood, including prescription drugs, recreational drugs, sex and work.

Work was like a drug because it was the only thing that I was sure of when everything else was unsure. Work was my only source of income. Without work there was no big city, no bigger world.

Even though I thought my enough was enough for me, sometimes I needed perfection and affirmation of my being. In those moments I had one friend who I could always call on and he would show up. Like a trained tiger, he would step up on the stool, on command.

One night I called him to show up and he did. Thinking about it now, I can relive every moment of that devastating night. He laughed hard and long and drank. I decided that night I wouldn't allow myself to get too drunk but to remain sober. After too much water, I had to make a needed sanitary stop.

On my way back to the living room, I heard the click from the lock of my front door.

My friend left without saying one word. My world crumbled into ten thousand little pieces of anger, shame, frustration, disbelief and hate.

I tried calling him until my phone battery was drained. I got dressed, went out and awoke the next morning in a pool of tears not knowing why.

Slowly, I replaced all of my enough for everyone's but myself ... literally pleasing my world and everything in it to get rid of the brokenness. The edges of my broken, splintered soul would cut into my skin letting me know I wasn't worthy.

Trapped in a maze, I searched for the stars to guide me out of it. I turned and kept running up against walls. No one understood me when I was calling and shouting, "Help me."

I'm was feeling so lost. I could hear voices and sense their fear but couldn't reach out to answer. My lips wouldn't move, my eyes wouldn't blink. I was a blank page. Frustration was piling up until the tears started rolling down my face onto the page, turning the notes into something. A sketch formed out of my mascara and tears as if the paper understood me more than I did. A heart, shaped out of my frustration and the stars I still could not see. My eyes were too blurry and I was not focused. I didn't look up for the stars ... why?

Standing on a crossroad, I only wanted to come out of this deep, dark disturbing reality. I needed a break the moment I realized I was drowning. I was trying to be a better person and I was trying to make a difference in different ways. Still my life was empty and I was never satisfied.

I found out that I had to break the cycle. The only way I could do that was through love. How could I use love when I don't know love myself?

Falling in love with me and accepting my flaws and my mistakes was and still is one of the hardest things to do. The thing about love is that it comes from within first, before you can be able to receive it.

We all have, at some time, a voice that tells us our mistakes and shortcomings. It tells us how we are not worthy and that we are not enough. It's time to mute it by loving ourselves.

I always tried to please everyone around me, to give 300% at work and to be my very best. All that giving, caring, doing, fixing and trying, led me to a high blood pressure attack on my 30th birthday. After a nice evening out, I came home and I had the attack in my shower.

I could see my life fast forwarding right in front of me. Being on the bathroom floor, I realized that the way I was living, wasn't going to work. I had to make some mayor changes.

I started prioritizing in my mind and making different choices regarding friendships, family and work. I had lost my faith in Jesus but lying on the floor, was the moment I had a realization. The one thing that always assured, guided and saved me in the past, was my faith and the love Jesus always showed me.

With baby steps, I began stepping out of my darkness into my renewed faith and light. The joy and happiness I experienced, I cannot describe with words.

I want you to know that you are enough regardless of your past or history. I want you to know that you matter the most ... without anyone else's opinion. I want you to know that there is always someone who cares for you, without a doubt. I want you to know that the only way to be you and stand your ground is with love, through faith and acceptance of yourself. I want you to know that you are not Anonymous.

## My Name is Anonymous

*I was bruised, beaten, buried and crushed.*

*The pain I felt was so severe nothing could take it away.*

*Not love, money, sex or things.*

*My life was glamorous ... for me.*

*Working out the way it should ... like a movie all parts were put together and rolls played well orchestrated ... by me.*

*But was it my life or was it my masterpiece?*

*Masterly pieced together, pieces MasterCard couldn't pay for.*

*Life like live action rolled out in front of me.*

*How could my mind play all those tricks on me, letting me believe that I was good?*

*Fooled by my masterly mind, buried under lies and deceit.*

*Lust and curiosity led me to believe that my salvation was in one night 'onlys.' Loneliness came in and hammered me down like a nail in a concrete wall ... impossible to go through.*

*Drugs made me believe that my lies were my reality.*

*Leading and misleading, misses and lost lonely souls to believe I was genuine.*

*Trademark stamped, originally sealed....
signed with a confession of a pitch black,
bruised heart.*

*How, how, how was it possible that after all
those years of knowing all those unruly false
misleads,*

*I believed and was convinced that they were
true.*

*I sat front row with a bottle of champagne
enjoying my free fall to my destiny ...
destruction.*

*My mirror was smeared with guilt, lies and
deceit.*

*Impossible to see my reflection, yet daily
putting on my makeup to make up for the
audience ... me.*

*What should have been homecoming became
operation clean house.*

*Not fully aware that someone was forcing
me to clean out my closet I was desperately
holding on and stacking up the skeletons.*

*The stinky smells hidden under the facade of
Cleanex and thick bleach. Rearranging them*

*so they could look a little brighter ... new and fresh.*

*The closet became too small and my back too weak to carry all these burdens.*

*Not fully aware of the facts that you already carried them for me.*

*There I was on my knees, not praying or fasting, but fighting to get on my feet and carry what you already did for me.*

*My name is Anonymous and I was bruised, beaten, buried and crushed under my sins.*

*But you came and bleached, washed and clothed me.*

*With a white linen cloth, without a blemish and spot, but I was never fully aware of the fact that it was so easy.*

*How could you choose me, knowing I would disappoint you over and over and over again?*

*How could a heart like mine be ever cleaned and shine. How?*

*I'm incomplete in this world.*

*But with you I'm complete*

*Fill my heart with your love and never let me desire a love that's not yours.*

*You've cleaned my smeared windows with love so it will shine bright*

*Showing others that light comes from within*

*My mirror you cleaned out with forgiveness.*

*You forgave me so who am I not to forgive.*

*Anonymous is dead because you called me by my name.*

*The one you gave me before my birth.*

*To all the ones who think they are anonymous.*

afi vrijdag

groen

I found my salvation in Christ.

# CHAPTER 3

# *You Gotta To Be Hungry*

Dr. Sonia Noel

25

I had so many questions in my mind travelling to Rhode Island for the first time on my way to the prestigious Brown University. Located in historic Providence, Rhode Island and founded in 1764, Brown University is the seventh-oldest college in the United States and a member of the Ivy League. I had seen pictures of the campus at Brown and it was huge and had very impressive architecture. Many famous people walked through those corridors. Personalities like John Fitzgerald Kennedy Jr., Emma Watson, Robert Edward "Ted" Turner III and many more.

I must admit I was very nervous to be the first Caribbean Designer to be invited there for a presentation on the Caribbean, during Caribbean Month. Also, it was an opportunity to showcase my collection. When I received the message asking if I would be interested in doing a presentation on the Caribbean, I was shocked because I knew no one at the university or in Rhode Island. I gave an affirmative response, then later received the official letter requesting my presence to present on Caribbean fashion as well as showcase my collection. All expenses would be covered. I was curious to know how I was selected so I asked the person who contacted me. She said when the decision was made to include Caribbean Fashion, they started researching designers from the region and my profile impressed them the most. This was an honour because from Jamaica in the north to Trinidad in the south, there are super talented designers.

I was travelling with my boyfriend at the time and he assured me that I would do well and everything would be more than fine. The first thing that happened was we got lost on the campus, although we had a map. We were laughing at ourselves and joking that the campus must be bigger that some villages. After calling Yanely Espanial, who was the contact person, we were directed to the correct location. We received a very warm welcome, which was encouraging. We were invited for a grand tour of the campus which was brilliant. I was assigned a very energetic assistant to get my collection ready for the show. We had a few hours to relax before the event and we certainly did much more than relax.

My friend and I had the most astonishing experience of real intimacy that made relaxation even better. It felt as if we were drifting into a trance and floating on clouds. Energy was generated with a nap and I felt ready for the evening proceedings.

During my presentation on Caribbean Fashion that evening, I was a bit nervous as the audience were extremely quiet. You could have heard a pin drop which made me even more nervous. I thought about myself, standing before an esteem audience, the same person with a big dream that most people thought was impossible. I got flashes of that little girl from the small mining town of Bartica who kept dreaming against the odds. Bartica is located on the Essequibo River which is the largest river in Guyana South America, and the largest river between the Orinoco and Amazon. That young girl who years ago stood in her grandma's yard looking at the kids from her school going to the Christmas party and wishing she could attend. Her mom could not afford a suitable dress for the party. That young girl who was not sure if milk would be available for her tea or if she would have tea at all. That young girl who walked the seven avenues and nine streets to sell pastries, cakes and buns. That young girl who enthusiastically knocked on doors asking if people wanted to buy pastries. Now that girl was standing on a campus that was bigger than her hometown.

Some days were better than others and I always tried to maintain a positive mindset. My WHY propelled me to stay positive because each slice of cake that was sold contributed to my family's finances since my dad had decided not to be supportive. It made me more determined, as the eldest child, to help mom take care of my other siblings. My self-discipline started way back, out of necessity. This was benefitting even at the time I was wrapping up my presentation to start the fashion display.

I could tell from the audience's reaction that they enjoyed my presentation. They were not the only ones because John was looking at me with great admiration and I was reassured that he was proud of me.

A young lady with an American accent came and hugged me with great excitement and she told me how proud she was to be Guyanese. I asked her where in Guyana was she from. She said, "My parents are from Guyana but after seeing you up there tonight I am proud to be Guyanese." That certainly boosted my confidence.

Driving back to NY the next day, I was on a natural high just thinking about my experience and the welcome I had received. I am a testimony of how dreams can come through. Our lives come down to the decisions we make as we get what we believe and not what we wish for. We are responsible for the choices we make. One of my favorite quotes is:

"Wanting something is not enough. You must hunger for it. Your motivation must be absolutely compelling in order to overcome the obstacles that will invariably come your way." - Les Brown

How hungry are you?

In 2005 I developed a hunger for a change after the devastating floods in Guyana. Walking into a space that used to be my beautiful showroom, work room and office was very depressing. My machines and fabric supply were under water and most of the contents in the showroom were destroyed. I took some photographs and returned to my home. Getting into my yard was challenging because the water was rising everywhere.

I looked at the pictures and thought, what a disaster! I was forced to stay in the house for a few days because of this catastrophic flood. It continued to rain heavily and in some areas, water hit record highs. The severe damage to low lying infrastructure, agriculture production, livestock and livelihood were devastating.

Epidemic diseases such as Leptospirosis, (also known as swineherd's disease, swamp fever, or mud fever) claimed lives. As waters receded, the likelihood of incidence of vector borne disease such as Dengue Fever increased. It was a distressing time for my beautiful homeland with the most hospitable people in the world. It was a dismal period for my family and I had to make a crucial decision with not much time.

I am action oriented and my thoughts were in over drive. I decided on two of my favourite countries where I had clients: Barbados and Suriname. In a few days, I visited my Dutch neighbour Suriname.

My first time there was almost two decades earlier and I instantly fell in love with this Dutch speaking country. The people almost mirrored the hospitality of Guyanese and the ladies were very sophisticated. I had an extensive clientele, including the then First Lady, Mrs. Elizabeth Venetiann. She was a phenomenal woman and I admired her humility. I respect people who are in powerful positions and can connect with the ordinary person. My next stop was Barbados where I also knew some people like veteran Barbadian designer and show producer, Betty West. She is an iconic figure who I met over two decades before and she had hosted some of the best fashion shows on the island. After one week on my mission trip, I decided Barbados would be my home few a few years.

Immediately after returning to Guyana I visited my mom to discuss my future plans since some included her. I told her of my plans to leave Guyana for a few years and needed her to assist in taking care of my children, Mariska and Shonta. Mom is very supportive and she said she would do whatever was necessary to assist me with my new plans. My two girls, were not thrilled with the news that they would have to return to Bartica for a while, without me. After living in the city for years and attending school, developing friendships I understood why they would feel that way. We all get to crossroads in life where we have to sacrifice something or someone.

It grieved my heart that I had to disrupt my children's lives but it was comforting that they would be with my mom who I trusted with my life. I had visited Barbados more than forty times prior to 2005 but this time it was different. I would be taking up residence on this beautiful island. Within a week, I rented a place on Maxwell Coast

Road, registered my business and began working on my business status at the Immigration Office.

I converted one of the rooms for my boutique because it was more economical since I would be starting over.

One month later, we had the official opening of Sonia Noel Designs with a fashion display on the lawns of my new residence. There was media coverage and attendance by some well know people on the island. The momentum was building at a rapid pace. I was travelling frequently back home in order to see my kids and fill orders since the manufacturing was still being done in Guyana. I also started travelling more to the Eastern Caribbean. The possibility of my children joining me sooner than later was my priority and my prayers intensified. Within six months, my prayers were answered and I was over the moon with joy and so was Mariska.

Shonta was very close to her great-grandma, Winifred, and the few months in Bartica had strengthened the bond they shared. She was not ready to leave yet which made me sad because I knew how much they loved each other. My grandma lived with us for years in Bartica and when Shonta was born she took great care of her. I actually credit a lot Shona's discipline to her.

I organized Mariska's Student visa and enrolled her in Urseline Convent School, which is a reputable private school on the island. She hit it off with the kids and teachers instantly.

She was looking forward to having fun on the beautiful beaches which is one of the things she had enjoyed while on holiday there many times, from the age of five.

Shonta decided to join us one year later and I tried enrolling her in St. Angella's School, with is the primary school to Urseline Convent. The head teacher told me, unfortunately, there was no space available for her because the class was at capacity. I loved the standards of both schools and the class rooms were not over crowded. I thought for a minute and asked her to please look at Shonta's report card from her previous school, in Guyana, before she made a decision. I respected the school's policies but I had to say something. I needed Shonta to be close to her sister because she was a bit shy, but super smart.

Her smartness paid off because when the Head Teacher read the report card, she said, "I need to make a call." Not sure who was at the other end of the line, I heard her say, "We need to make an exception for this child because her report card is excellent." My baby got into the school on her on merit and not because of who her mom was. The combination of her brilliance and God's grace could only produce positive results and I felt blessed.

I was a bit worried that the move would affect her Grade 6 Examination results, which was a year away. Adjusting to a new environment sometimes could be difficult and result in a change in behaviour. Shonta requested visits to two top schools on the island to make a decision of the one she would attend after the Grade six Exams. After looking at both Harrison College and Queens College, she decided on Queens

College which was her favourite. QC was on her results slip the next year and I soon realized that my daughter was as hungry as or probably even hungrier than I was.

I can, without a doubt, say that moving to Barbados when I did was one of the best decisions I ever made.

I constantly challenge myself with the possibilities of what's possible. I did it over two decades ago, moving from Bartica to the capital city, Georgetown then in 2005, when I made that decision to move to Barbados to live. There's always something so exciting about new beginnings. I must say that although there were challenges, I had a lot of faith and was determined to make things work. It pushed me to grow faster than I anticipated. Not only me but my daughters as well. Both girls were involved in sports and other extracurricular activities at their schools. Outside of school, they would go to polo, sailing and spent time at the beach with friends. The atmosphere assisted them in becoming well rounded and confident young ladies which propelled them to do exceptionally well in their studies and now in their careers.

While living in Barbados, I challenged myself to host the first Guyana fashion weekend. I returned home and put a team together of people I thought were visionaries. To my surprise, most of them thought the idea was too big for Guyana and I was crazy to even think of it. Well, I didn't mind being called crazy and I used the negatives as fuel for the engine to get me to my destination. Last year, we celebrated ten years of Guyana Fashion Week.

There is a saying that if you have never been called crazy, your dreams are not big enough. I certainly don't mind being labelled as crazy.

# CHAPTER 4

# *Knowing Your Purpose*

Linda Felix-Johnson-MS. Psychology

'Loving the life you are living is the realest and truest demonstration of purpose.'

There is not a day in the last 10 years that I haven't had thoughts about the fulfillment I feel on the road to discovering my purpose. One of the first things I did was to gauge the degree of satisfaction I derive from attending to the key areas of my life in assessing my levels of fulfillment. I realized that loving my current life and setting goals big enough to live my purposeful life WERE IMPORTANT TO MY SUCCESSES. THEREFORE, I reorganized my planning and increased my doing. In the process of achieving MY set goals, I discovered a passion to do more.

I worked at the World Trade Center for more than a decade before my life changed drastically on September 11, 2001 ('9/11'). While I (and, what turned out to be, hundreds of people) were entomb in the rubble and trying to dig out to safety, I prayed and hoped that I would be given a second chance, but my reasons were personal. At that time, I was caring for my ailing mother, and my two daughters were in college and middle school. I felt that my children still needed their mother's guidance, and if given the opportunity, I WOULD CHANGE MANY

THINGS. Through, what I call, divine intervention, the others and I managed to get out to safety. WHILE DOING SO, we saw the bodies of people who unfortunately lost their lives.

The next three months after this eventual life-altering experience were quite difficult, but I felt this was my very second chance for a reason, though not knowing what it really was. HOWEVER, I knew I would not be returning to the rat race of Wall Street - the popular regard for the environment where the event occurred.

AFTER MY HARROWING EXPERIENCE, I took some time to heal both emotionally and psychologically. A chance meeting to discuss an issue at my grand-daughter's school with a man who would later become my friend and mentor, the late Dr. Walter Kyte, led me to becoming an educator with the NYC Department Of Education working with Special Education students. I had my 'ah-ha moment'. You see, I never felt I had the tolerance or patience to work with children, but Dr. Kyte recognized the advocate in me that I, myself, even did not see.

Working with Special and General Education high school students became both rewarding and fulfilling. I found myself advocating for those students because they are sometimes treated negatively, but I held the firm feeling that all children should be given an opportunity to reach their highest potential. I would spend as much time after school with 9th. & 10th grade students with reading deficiencies bringing them up to the grades' levels. The English teacher and I saw the positive difference the intervention made in the students. In one case, a 9th grade student, reading below the 1st grade level was acting out his frustration in the class room because he could not identify two-letter words. My intervention elevated his reading skills to the 7th grade level within one year, allowing him to noticeably walk around the halls with newfound confidence and high self-esteem, and later taking up leadership roles in his class. In addition, there were three special education students who benefited from the program at the time, allowing two of them to attend college.

## **Finding Passion**

Working on Wall Street was just a job; it paid the bills, but I hadn't discovered my purpose, my passion, my mission in life until I worked with those students and observing the difference my intervention made in their lives. I knew I had found my purpose. I came home every evening trying to find different ways to motivate them, and could not wait to get into the class room the next morning. Sometimes it takes another person to see things you are trying to deny in yourself, or as I communicate to people in my conferences, "Stop being scared to step out of your comfort zone."

My journey was not easy. Along the way there were lots of obstacles. Indeed, there were times when I felt the need to 'press pause' and reevaluate my path, but other forces always redirected my thoughts and actions. I call it divine intervention because I believe that when we pray and ask God for guidance, we should follow the path he has prepared for us. I decided to follow that path and even though the valleys were sometimes low or as I say "climbing on the rough side of the mountain", I had faith that I was on the right path. I found my passion aligned with the issues of which I wholesomely cared about, such as social justice, advocacy for women's and children's rights (especially those within the inner city and students considered differently-abled; as well as seniors who I strongly believe should enjoy respectful love and care in the sunset years of life. Discovering what I was passionate about, I had to, subsequently, formulate a plan and become laser focused on how to achieve those objectives.

> *'I have come to believe that each one of us has a personal calling that's as unique as a fingerprint – and that the best way to succeed is to discover what you love and then find a way to offer it to others in the form of service, working hard, and also allowing the energy of the universe to lead you'. - Oprah*

## **Plan Of Action**

I began my journey taking baby steps developing an after school program Exclusive Community Literacy Foundation, Inc.) to assist students and adults with reading deficiencies. I am a true believer that education is power and, information is power, also. However, based on my interaction with the parents of those students, I realized that the parents were not receiving or understanding the Special Education System due to a combination of issues which led to confusion. I believe in straight talk and, as we all know, that can get you into trouble sometimes. Nevertheless, when you truly believe in something you have to forgo the repercussions and do what's right, at times.

It was the perception of most parents and students in the special education realm that a Special Education High School diploma is the same as a standard High School diploma OR Regents Diploma and they did not have to apply themselves; just do the bear minimum, and that credential will enable them to get a job or probably be used for college admission. A related statement by a student - whom I will call, Sam - propelled me to share the reality with the parents and students concerning the credentials of which they were not aware of and did not want to hear. He said, "I will be the first to graduate from high school in my family", and he said this with pride referring to the IEP diploma. You see, these students were in the 9th and 10th grades with low or no reading and comprehension skills, and they were just moving through the school

system thinking that they just had to be 'present'. It was akin to just attending school for four years, and then leave with abysmal skills. That saddened me' so I decided to do something about it. I painfully advised the students and their parents that an IEP diploma just means that the owner merely attended high school, but did not necessarily achieve the credentials to apply for a low wage job, apply for higher education or enroll in a technical school. Additionally, I spent time informing the parents that after spending four years in high school their children will have to enroll in a Test Assessing Secondary Completion program (TASC) which replaced the General Education Development (GED) examination - a testing process, in my opinion, that is for persons like me who came to the US as an adult seeking higher education and needing to verify knowledge in core content areas equivalent to that of graduating high school seniors. Their responses were of disbelief; thus underscoring my mantra of 'knowledge and information is power'. That created some major concerns, but since I believe that benefits outweigh risks, I made a conscious decision to continually counsel them. The students asked a lot of questions and most of them began applying themselves purposefully, striving to receive either a standard High School Diploma or a High School Regents Diploma.

'We should never be afraid to speak the truth to power in defense of the powerless because without the truth we become powerless' - Unknown

I joined organizations with missions and objectives that advocated for the voiceless and less fortunate, while volunteering, initiating, coordinating, and conducting several programs aimed at benefitting school-aged children, seniors and women's empowerment in the US, Guyana & Trinidad and several other countries. I learned to become non-negotiable over what I felt was important to change lives for better outcomes, while staying flexible listening and learning how to have realistic expectations.

## Living with Passion and Purpose

It is sometimes difficult to objectively evaluate oneself, but I was self-motivated to do just that and the result was absolutely rewarding. With two daughters now in college, I decided to wait until they were finished with their studies before PURSUING a degree of my own. As soon as my younger daughter Keshia completed her Master's degree, both she and her older sister Keisha told me, "Mom it's your turn", and my turn it was. Having a clear vision of what I wanted to accomplish, I was able to earn my Bachelor's degree in two and one half years and my Masters in Psychology with a specialization in Early Childhood and Adolescent Development and Mental Health and Family Counseling. I later received certification as a Literacy Specialist in order to be able to better serve my students, and later began serving as a certified Public Speaking Trainer & Facilitator. You see, I was focused on acquiring the tools to appropriately assist others. In effect, I decided what I needed for myself; aware that someone can live their purpose without the acquisition of higher education. It's just that need to find what makes you happy and do it to the best of your ability. You are the only one who gets to define your purposeful life.

*'It's time to start living the life you imagined.'*

*-Henry James, American novelist and playwright*

On one of my many trips to my hometown of Linden, Guyana as coordinator of the annual medical and educational missions, I founded the idea to conduct a forum for women only where the attendees can openly discuss issues that affect and impede their progress. Upon my return to the US, I invited a few friends (who eventually became co-founders) Bernita Primo, Wenda Hutson, Ismay Griffith and the late Guliana Jacobs to join forces and volunteer their services to this noble women's community-development idea. I founded and named the new organization **Women Of Mission International, Inc. (WOMI)** which has been providing a wide range of services and programs to include Sponsor A Student; Sponsor A School; Sponsor A Program; Students Back Pack Program; Literacy & Mentorship Programs, higher education Scholarship Program and the launch of a Seniors Day Program. WOMI currently has a chapter in Linden, Guyana which is led by Chairwoman Camille Cummings, as well as Wanda Richmond, Lulu Bynoe, Trudy Scott, Monica Higgins and other phenomenal women. (www.womenofmission.com)

I frequently speak on leadership responsibility and the importance of being committed to motivating our young people. I am committed to assisting others in discovering their leadership skills through group facilitation, motivational speeches and workshops/seminars. In addition, I attend and

49

participate in community activities speaking to students and parents about the importance of education in whatever field they wish to pursue, and imploring upon parents the need to assume an active role in their children's lives and education. I am passionate about the importance of educating low income, inner city and differently abled youths/students.

Also, I am the Chief Executive Officer of SistaSoul Productions Company (SSPC) - a multifaceted creative arts enterprise producing and staging theatrical, fine-arts, media, literary and cultural presentations and workshops. I am the mother of two beautiful and accomplished daughters Keisha and Keshia. I also have an adorable grand-daughter, Khala, and a special niece, Angela who has become a successful businesswoman.

I strive to improve myself to help others, and I believe that my life is more enriched when I 'pay it forward'. In addition to living my purposeful life, I am actively involved in caring for my 96 year old ailing mother who lives with me in Brooklyn, NY. I spend my frugal spare time indulging in reading, networking, listening to music and spending quality time with family.

I thank God every day for giving me the health and strength to help others, and my children for their unconditional support. My favorite quote consists of the lyrics from a Dianne Ross song, "Reach out and touch somebody's hand, Make this world a better place, if you can."

You too can change your life and live your purpose beginning today!!

> *'We may encounter many defeats but*
> *we must not be defeated'*
> *-Maya Angelou*

One Love!

## Questions to ask yourself to live more purposefully

- When have you been happiest in your life?
- What has made you truly proud of yourself?
- What qualities do you most admire in other people?
- What makes you feel alive and energized?
- How happy do you feel on an everyday basis?
- What is one change that could make your life happier?
- What 'shoulds' are overriding your 'wants and needs'?
- If you can change one thing about your life, what would it be?

# CHAPTER 5

# *Receiving To Give*

Ediclia Bastardo de Persaud

I have faced many challenges in my life and I have conquered them all, I have come out of all of them. Although I was born and grew up in humble communities, I always dreamed big and with optimism. When I graduated from college, my first job was at a university, many of my students were older than me. My colleagues who graduated with me started working in secondary schools and told me that it was better to acquire experiences in high school to be able to work in universities with adults later. I, on the contrary, did not think it was difficult to enter the university labour field, for me it was a challenge to face. My first experience as a university teacher was extraordinary, learning, vast and enriching.

During the development of my career, I realized that discipline, perseverance and constancy are the infallible weapons of success. Although I participated in multiple activities, I managed to exceed all of them since I gave a lot of effort, discipline and above all, passion to everything I did. College life helped me not only in my professional training but also in my spiritual, social and personal life. From the beginning of my career, I participated and worked as president of a Christian youth group, called JUCEM, Juventud Universitaria Cristiana Evangelica Misionera, whose functions were to evangelize the university community, both inside and outside the campus. We also did missionary and social work in villages, very poor neighbourhoods and indigenous communities. The work with JUCEM allowed me to travel frequently in the fulfilment of my duties as president of the group, generally to do missionary and social work.

Our job was to bring some relief to so much need that prevailed in the communities. Primarily we carried medical and dental assistance, basic medicine supply, clothing, and school items, etc. To obtain all this help, we required a good dose of work, effort and above all a good logistical management. Thanks to the perseverance of the participants who were students of the university and the cooperation of the university authorities, drugstores, health centers and pharmacies, we could carry out these important journeys of help.

The most rewarding and extraordinary activities were the trips to indigenous communities in the states of Monagas, Delta Amacuro and Bolívar, some of which preserved their culture and customs. Sometimes we had to spend several days living with the inhabitants, sharing their customs, gastronomy and activities. It was quite exciting, but sometimes it became a challenge to have to do everything and to cover basic needs without electricity and in precarious health conditions (for us). In short, we spent several days in full and direct contact with nature, moving from one community to another in very small boats, often devoid of motor, learning from true masters, our indigenous brothers. It was so rewarding to arrive at the communities, see all the movements and attention that they showed us as they sang the national anthem in their language to welcome us.

At the beginning of my career, I had many financial shortages since the only sustenance I had was my father, who died a few months before starting my university journey. My mother, who had never worked outside the home, had to start working by cleaning offices and schools. Before starting my university career, I sometimes helped my mother with her job.

I went through so many needs and deficiencies that on many occasions I dressed in the clothes of my mother, who was a bit thicker than me. Her feet were delicate and small, which is why I often damaged her shoes because I wore a larger size.

I want to relate one of the many experiences that showed me the greatness of God's love and faithfulness in my life. One of the many times I had to return to the university, which was three hours away from my hometown, in the beautiful Maturin, Monagas State, I had come home to spend the weekend and visit my family, especially my sick father. It was usually very difficult for my family to get the money for me to cover my basic needs, such as: food, transportation and the payment of the residence (place where I rented a room shared with another student).

I had to return to the university but my mother did not have the money. Both of us were distressed because I had exams to attend.

In front of my mother's workplace there was a park and I sat there with one of my brothers to wait for my mother. I was sad and upset because I wanted to pursue my career with all my heart, but it was going uphill because of my precarious economic condition. I started talking alone, with myself and with God. I remember the words I said, "God, it's not fair, there are so many people with so much money and they do not want to study or have goals in life. Instead I, who want to study, prepare myself and to reach so many goals, do not have a penny, to pay the passage to go to the university." Those were my words, among other complaints and reflections. I did not realize that behind me was a lady, a little older than my mother. She was completely dressed in denim as she approached and greeted me kindly. She asked me for the newspaper of the day, which I had in my hands and we began to talk. (She still remembers everything we talked about). She told me that she had unintentionally heard what I had said a few moments ago and she asked me about my studies. I told her, with great emotion, that I wondered about my career, how much I liked my field of study and thank God my grades were excellent. I never imagined what would happen to me with that nice lady. Her name is Ernestina de Sánchez. Her husband had died three months ago, and she was a professional with an important position, with good income, very altruistic and kind. She told me that I caught her attention while speaking so deeply of my determination and passion.

When her husband died, on the deathbed she promised him that she would look for a person to support her needs, a person with truly precarious needs. She had been three months looking and that day, when listening to me, she found who she was looking for. From that day on, she helped me to pay for my studies, provided me with food, transportation, clothes, supplies and necessary books, as well as the payment of my residence. My dear Mrs. Ernestina is one of the most special people I have ever met and I thank infinitely my good God for having used her. She made me promise that I would not tell anyone until I graduated, only my mother knew and few of my siblings. She said that only God and I should know about the help. This experience was one of many that once again showed me the immense love of God and corroborated with me that God certainly had a great purpose for me. I consider myself a lucky woman, since, in my life, many times, angels like Mrs. Ernestina appeared to help me and work in my favour.

Another of the means for my sustenance was the part-time job I got, months later, teaching in primary schools. Every day I woke up with the firm intention of being happy and gave the best of myself. Although circumstances sometimes seemed impossible, I always maintained an optimistic attitude and faith. At the end of my university journey, I not only obtained the degree that accredits me as a professional, but I obtained the best grades, earning the first place for my academic index. In addition to my professional training, I grew as a person and strengthened moral and spiritual values that enriched me as a human being.

Working with JUCEM allowed me to fraternize with many students and professors of the university. We met twice a week to pray, worship and plan the evangelistic, missionary, social and academic work. We always had a busy agenda with enough work. Many times I did not have enough time to study and my classmates worried about my academic welfare. I organized myself in such a way that I always got excellent grades because I had to set an example as a good leader.

There were too many extraordinary experiences during my university career, especially for the missionary service through JUCEM. When I graduated I did not return to my hometown immediately. I had to have six more months of training and was one of the most loyal members of the group to continue leading the work.

Back in Barcelona, my city, I started looking for a job, and quickly got into a university in which I worked parallel with my work in a public secondary school. To opt for a government job, I participated in a national merit contest and won the first place. It was an honour for me. I worked hard and lovingly, treating my students with a lot of patience. They were extraordinary years of which I've kept beautiful memories since it was my first stage as a professional teacher. I always trusted God, asking for wisdom to face each challenge and I learnt a lot with each experience.

Years later, I renewed communication with my present husband, whom I met at the beginning of my career. My husband is of Guyanese nationality and we got married in Guyana in 1999, the last year of the 20th century. It is already 19 years that God has allowed us to live and share together. Our first daughter, Tatiana was born in Guyana 18 years ago. After a couple of years, we returned to Venezuela where we had our other two girls, Shaneeza, 15 and

Chritsibell, 13. They are my most precious treasures.

A couple of years later we returned to Guyana and started working again with the Embassy of Venezuela, since I already had experience with the Diplomatic Mission. I worked for 5 consecutive years. The first three as a local official assuming different responsibilities, from a Spanish teacher to coordinating counselor of the cultural development area. I also performed other functions that the position of Specialist Professor allowed me to assume. My work allowed me to plan, design and execute and monitor academic, social and cultural development programs. They were enriching responsibilities, which allowed me vast learning and significant growth both professionally and personally. I made an excellent team with the mission chief and other employees and officials of the embassy.

Two years before finishing my period in the embassy, the head of mission proposed that I continue as a diplomatic officer, for which I had to travel to Caracas, Venezuela to receive intensive training. It was a wonderful experience that allowed me to interact with a group of colleagues who were then sent to different countries of the world to represent our country through the different embassies and consulates of Venezuela. The learning obtained complemented the acquired experience through the work I had been doing. When I arrived at the Venezuelan Institute for Culture and Cooperation - IVCC in Georgetown, I understood the great responsibility I had in my hands, the work I was about to do was not the same to what I had done up until then, I knew again that it was a great challenge that I had to face with the wisdom and human vocation with which God has blessed me. I had to design a 9-level Spanish language teaching program, from Basic I to Conversational Level. That program is still used in the IVCC to teach Spanish.

The Social Development Area was born as a response to the need for solving social problems that affected the most depressed female population, especially women in situations of abuse and special needs. This area was designed to promote social programs aimed at increasing the overall well-being of the population and improving the quality of life in the community, through responsible and participatory management. This fostered social inclusion.

I had the opportunity to meet and share with extraordinary, valuable and talented women. Many came to the IVCC to participate in the various training programs that provided them with the necessary training for productive work. Others served as volunteer facilitators and others as special guests, who supported us in the different activities and with motivational speeches for the participants, mostly women. For many of them, coming to the IVCC represented 'everything' in their lives, because before the training, their lives were limited to the routine of the house, without hope of growth as people or as professionals. Others suffered from family abuse at the hands of their partners and other family members. Our programs not only provided them with training in the area of professional development, but also offered them the proper guidance to cope with the emotional and family situations they were facing.

One of the experiences that I remember the most, which left me with a great learning was to work with young people, women and men with special needs. I remember that the courses were dictated on Saturdays. I could not wait for Saturdays to come to share with this 'truly special' group, which gave me an inexplicable joy and gratification. There was a woman who attended a flower-making course with her two daughters with special needs, both women were in their twenties. The girls had grown up in the absence of the father figure and they were also very poor. After obtaining the second certificate for participation in the courses, the state of health of the mother worsened and a few months later, she died. It was a devastating blow for the family, especially for the daughters who fortunately were helped by relatives. Because they had trained and acquired skills to make flowers and other arrangements, they could help themselves financially by selling the product of their work. There were many experiences that left traces in me during the time I worked in the development of each program.

"I thank God for each one of the people who in one way or another have impacted each stage of my life's history. I also thank my beloved family, who has been with me in the most intense and enriching experiences. Thanks to you, hoping that at least my words will help you to find yourself, value yourself and follow your true path.

In retrospect, I can say that God has allowed me to carry out different positions, from teaching in a school to representing my country as a Charge D'Affaires in a diplomatic mission. In all cases it was necessary to have great responsibility and leadership. All the family, work, personal and missionary experiences have allowed me to become the person I am today. I think I still have a lot to learn and share, remembering the famous words of Jesus Christ, "It is more blessed to give than to receive."

# CHAPTER 6
## *Freedom Always Comes With A Price Tag*

# Women Across Borders – with a mission

## Isabelle D Ncgobo.

South Africa's musical icon and jazz legend, died at the age of 78 due to complications with prostate cancer. He had received many awards during his lifetime in recognition of his musicianship and global contributions in the struggle to end Apartheid. This was the news I woke up to on the morning of January 23, 2018.

Deeply saddened, I started reflecting and counting my blessings on the numerous times I had the opportunity to be in the presence of this legendary musical icon. Interacting with Hugh Masekela, affectionately known as "Bra Hugh, the father of South African Jazz," was always an uplifting, encouraging, informative and musically, an entertaining experience. "Bra Hugh" was a pioneer and liberator who gave a voice to the plight of black South Africans and exposed the atrocities and circumstances black people in their native land had to endure. Those who were tried were often banished, or imprisoned for life, like Nelson Mandela who was released from prison on February 12, 1990.

I remember that day like it was yesterday. My husband and I woke earlier than usual that morning, the day of Nelson Mandela's release from Robben Island where he spent 18 of his 27 years in prison.

Glued to my seat I watched television and waited with the world in anticipation to see Nelson Mandela walk a free man. It was a bitter-sweet moment for me because it made me realize that freedom came at a prize.

As I watched the release of Nelson Mandela with millions of people around the world, I got flashback memories of when I was a child around seven or eight years old. My grandfather would often tell me stories about Nelson Mandela. He would share stories of how Nelson Mandela and his comrades would come in the middle of the night to sit at his shebeen in Sophiatown and discuss politics. A shebeen in those days was basically selling liquor without a permit at your house. This reminds me of a song called 'Kwulesa mama,' sung by the late Miriam Makeba and written by Dorothy Masuka with musical composition done by Hugh Masekela. The song is very telling because it explains how black kids would keep a watch out for police to come raid their houses while their parents were selling liquor in their houses   Kwulesa means 'hurry mama, please don't let them get you.' Selling liquor was another way for impoverished blacks to combat poverty. The liquor from your house was banned because the Apartheid government feared it when black people had gatherings anywhere, so they put a curfew, declaring Marshall Law on its black citizens.

Sophiatown, also known as Kofifi was a suburb of Johannesburg South Africa. It was a legendary black cultural hub that was destroyed under Apartheid. It was the Epi-centre of politics, jazz and blues during the 1940s and 1950s and produced some of South Africa's most famous writers, musicians, politicians and artists.

As I continued to watch the day's event unfold on television and watching Nelson Mandela walking in the street of Cape Town now a free man.  I noticed the thousands of black youth standing on the side of the roads cheering "Viva Nelson Mandela Viva," most of them still in their school uniforms.

A significant and powerful moment came when Nelson Mandela walked hand in hand with Winnie. They both raised their right arms with clenched fists saluting "Black Power.'

At that moment my mind went racing back to June 16, 1976. It was my first year in high school. Six months into the school calendar year, there was a call for a school boycott. Senior students were taking over the school for a week to hold rallies and protest. On that fateful morning, Black students, all across the nation, were going to boycott and fight for equal education and do away with what was called Bantu education and the laws that made it mandatory for students to do subjects in Afrikaans. This is the language that black students viewed as the "language of the oppressors." Sitting behind our desks, we waited to hear what our senior student had to say as he nervously paced up and down the classroom. I looked out through the open window at one point and felt a light winter breeze over my face, but before I could enjoy the moment, I heard three loud knocks on our classroom door. Suddenly, the door swung open and the senior student jumped through the window. A policeman and a dog chased after him and chaos erupted. More policemen stormed into the classroom and teargas was dispersed everywhere. Within seconds my eyes were burning and my chest hurting. It was hard to breathe. Somebody handed me a wet cloth to cover my nose and mouth, then I heard the word Run"! Without thinking twice, I grabbed my friend's hand and ran towards the door. To my surprise there were dozens of policemen outside chasing and hitting students with sjamboks. Some of us who managed to break away started running across the soccer fields towards our neighbourhood. My grandmother's house was not far from the school. She described the scene as "looking like a war zone." Many students hid out at my grandma's house until everything calmed down and police left the streets of our neighbourhood.

Meanwhile, all hell had broken loose and turned violent and deadly in Soweto

Township. We learned through news on the radio that unarmed students across Soweto took to the streets and marched to Orlando Stadium for a peaceful gathering to protest against Bantu Education. They were stopped by police and met with brutality that shocked the world. Soweto turned into a tragedy where a young student named Hector Peterson was the first black student shot and killed by police.

Public transportation was halted that day because the shooting and killings of unarmed students sparked massive uprising that soon spread to more urban and rural areas throughout South Africa. People who commuted with public transportation to and from work or college were given orders to wait until further notice.

My sister came home late that night telling us how the South African armed forces were everywhere in downtown Johannesburg ensuring order.

Watching the evening news and seeing the bloody images on TV was heart-wrenching. Going to bed that night and falling asleep wasn't easy. I tossed and turned all night, playing the day's event over and over in my head, trying to make sense of what happened. There were no easy answers. All I knew was that Soweto's school kids died in the name of freedom while fighting for a better education. My life changed forever that day. When something negative happens to you as a young child, that experience stays with you for life. For the first time, at the age of thirteen, I understood what it meant to be a black child born and raised in a systematic Apartheid South Africa.

Watching Nelson Mandela on TV now a free man, waving to the crowds smiling, and walking hand in hand with Winnie Mandela I began thinking of how I met my husband .

I remember the first time we met when I was performing at a music festival in Soweto. I noticed this dark and handsome man on the other side of the stage staring at me. I was waiting to enter the stage with a solo I had choreographed. The music came on and it was my turn to get on stage and perform my solo. Somewhere in my solo there was a pause in the music, based on the choreography and I had to freeze through that pause. It was during that freeze that our eyes met because he was standing slightly off-stage watching me dance. I believe that it was love at first sight.

Two weeks had passed since that day and one afternoon I got a call from a friend inviting me to an opening of a new recreation center. It was a Saturday and I had free time, so I decided to go. I got to the center and the first person to welcome me at the door was this man that I locked eyes with two weeks earlier at a festival in Soweto. He escorted me into the studio where the party was being held. Music played and he asked me to dance with him. Without hesitation I plunged into the moment, moved with it and joined him in the dance. It was a dance of seduction and it felt good.

From that moment on, we became close and started dating. He was from Soweto and I lived 20 miles South of Soweto. He would sometimes accompany me to my dance performances or visit me on TV sets. We would always make reference to the fact that not enough black dancers were given the opportunity to perform at the venues or on TV shows. It was because I would always be one of two black dancers or the only black dancer amongst white dancers.

Ballet, contemporary dance and jazz were my training. I guess you would call me fortunate because in Apartheid South Africa, you were only considered a professional dancer when you could master those three dance styles. That was the expected criteria for a so called professional dancer. Having mastered those dance forms, I could at least audition for the best high paying shows. If you opt to dance for an institutionalized dance company, you could do well as a white dancer because you are guaranteed principal roles if you are good. That opportunity was never awarded to black dancers no matter how great they were. The best roles would always go according to your skin colour first rather than your skills, and if you were lucky to get some sort of lead role was because you were just that damn good. Unfortunately, the colour of your skin would still play a role because you would get the shine but not the dime. In other words, you would get paid far less than a white dancer performing that same role as lead dancer. That was the law of the land.

Dating my husband who was my boyfriend at the time allowed me the opportunity to go with him to ANC (African National Congress) rallies. He was born and raised in Soweto, Orlando West. The same neighbourhood where Nelson Mandela, Winnie Mandela, Walter Sisulu and Desmond Tutu lived. It was also in my husband's neighbourhood where the first student got shot and killed during the Soweto uprising. The corner of Vilakazi Street is the most famous street in Soweto and all of South Africa because from that very same street also birthed two Nobel Prize Laureates, Nelson Mandela and Archbishop Desmond Tutu.

"Stability and peace in our land will not come from the barrel of a gun," he said, "because peace without justice is an impossibility." Those were the words of Desmond Tutu who became the first black person appointed as the Anglican Dean of Johannesburg in 1975. He was awarded the Nobel Prize in recognition of "the courage and heroism shown by black South Africans.

Living with my grandmother also meant going to church every Sunday whether you liked it or not. Desmond Tutu was one of the deacons at our church, the Anglican Church. My grandmother also joined a women's league at our church and they would often come together and discuss church and politics. They would reminiscent on the march of August 9th, 1956 where my grandmother along with 20.000 women of all races marched to the Union building in Pretoria to protest the introduction of the Apartheid Pass Laws Act for black women. Now dubbed "Women's Day," a national holiday in South Africa. She would always encourage me to work hard and do my best and once I've kicked the doors open, break down barriers and walls, to remember whose shoulders I stand on. She urged me to keep the doors open to invite others to come in because freedoms were bought at a price.

So as I continued watching the release of Nelson Mandela on the morning of February 12, 1990 as it played out on the TV. CNN broadcast the response from world leaders concerning Mandela's release. For the first time, South Africans realized the nature of Mandela's statue around the world. I was convinced that change had come to South Africa as Nelson Mandela was now a free man.

Three months after Nelson Mandela's release from prison, we got a phone call from Zindzi Mandela, the youngest daughter of Winnie and Nelson Mandela. She asked for our dance company, Soweto Street Beat, to do a welcome home performance, in honour of Madiba, at a family picnic in Soweto.

Soweto Street Beat Dance Theatre was the first black dance company in South Africa, which was co-founded by my husband, Peter Ngcobo, and I in 1989. We had the honour to meet Nelson Mandela. I told him that our dance company had an invitation to tour the US. That's very good he said, "Go and represent South Africa well, teach them who we are as South Africans and never forget where you come from'." I have never forgotten those words.

In 1994 Nelson Mandela was elected South Africa's first black president and the country became a democratic and free. Many people paid a price tag for freedom. Nelson Mandela fought a good fight, finished the race, and made his mark in history the way he wanted to be remembered.

Soweto Street Beat Dance Theatre moved to the USA, in 1992, and represented Africa in the 1996 Olympic Games. The Theatre also performed at the Cultural Olympiad in 2018 and is still the only South African black dance company in the USA.

The Apartheid regime may have robbed black South Africans from equal education and opportunities in South Africa, but they could not take away the dance, the music, the culture and the spirit. That spirit of Ubuntu.

# CHAPTER 7

# *"When your imaginations are manifested"*

Christine Neblett

83

I often wonder why anyone should have limiting belief in oneself. It is so amazing how I enjoy the fruits of living my dreams daily and all I want to do is share my stories over and over to inspire others that they too can live their dreams. The life I enjoy can best be described as a dream world and sometimes I want to pinch myself into reality. From the day I walked pass Wall Street, I envisioned working in that same building, developing a team of over 3,000 individuals in my down-line, as a rookie in MLM, and operating my own shipping and procurement business. I have accomplished all that and more by having a dream, a winning mindset and a steadfast determination which inevitably lead me to the success I now enjoy.

In September 2004, as I was getting ready to end my temporary project/assignment with the Caribbean Tourism Organization, I left for lunch and decided to browse the area surrounding downtown Manhattan with more emphasis on Wall Street. As I walked passed 60 Wall Street, I could only imagine myself walking out of that building like all the other important looking individuals in their suits and nicely dressed business oriented attire.

I proceeded to the nearest food establishment and purchased my lunch. As I was eating, all I could think of was, what I needed to do the land myself a job with that company. I therefore decided the action I needed to take was to inquire which company occupies the location. So, I immediately packed my lunch to head back to the front desk to see the security officer and to my surprise I found out that several companies occupied that location. With much determination, I asked her for the human resources department contact information to the largest company of the many companies and was greeted with an alternative. The female security officer offered me an option to return the next day and she would provide me with the necessary information to the "Temp Agency" that staffs most of the companies occupying that location. The following day at 1:00 p.m. couldn't come fast enough for me to take my lunch walk over to 60 Wall

Street. I collected the torn piece of paper, hurried over to the Au bon Pain restaurant to settle my anxious nerves and call Monique at the Staffing Agency.

That day I began to have the real experience of dreaming and bringing my dream world alive. I was immediately scheduled for an interview with the agency where they tested my proficiency in using Microsoft Office and typing speed. One week later I completed my assignment with CTO and was now ready to move on to my next career move. I called Monique to let her know I was available as we agreed and she was so happy to have me start my first temporary assignment with Deutsche Bank.

My first assignment lasted 2 weeks covering someone's vacation. Due to my work ethics and desire to go the extra mile I landed another assignment in the same department for 6 months, then another for 3 months which finally led to my permanent position, allowing me to live a dream.

December 2009, again began another dream opportunity when I was introduced to Multi-

Level Marketing in a very peculiar manner. At a party in Atlanta, a lady named Carol asked me if I knew anyone who would like to drop 3 sizes in 10 minutes. As unusual as it may have seem, I was the one who wanted that deal. I quickly responded, "She's standing in front of you", and that was the beginning of my MLM experience. Anything mastered has a learning pattern attached so if I wanted to master MLM I had to be willing to learn how to and apply what was taught. One pioneer in the industry would say, "If you are going to be a copy-cat, try copying from the right cat."

I did as was instructed and followed the proven system, got on all the calls, bombarded my friend Lynn and my co-workers to try the experience and then I got burnt out. No more friends and family members to "harass" according to what some of them would have explained my persistence to be.

Now, I found myself at a cross-road, whether to continue pressing forward or to quit. We all know, winners never quit and if I had any chance of succeeding I needed to try again and again until it worked. In my frustration, I decided pay my church a visit one morning, just to have some alone time in the pews to pray and meditate on the way forward. After praying I sat there and began to dream of myself standing in a room with hundreds of people who were eager to learn of my opportunity. I could see them coming to me for answers to their many issues and myself responding favourably. I then, got lost in the mood that was beginning to feel real to me.

The following day I made my plan to grow my organization, starting with a visit to Guyana then to Antigua and local showcasing. My first showcase in Guyana occurred in a small room at Main Street Plaza, the second was at a school location in an area called Queenstown in Guyana. However, with the combination of the individuals I met along the way with the small-scale meeting I expanded to our first Super Saturday event in half of the Savanah Suite at Pegasus Hotel.

It was at that first Super Saturday held at the Pegasus Hotel. I encouraged my team members and attendees to join my dreaming and visionary exercise by looking in the direction of the wall that had divided the Savanah Suite into two. I asked them to imagine that the wall was removed and the entire area was fully occupied. October of that year, my team and I packed the Savanah suites and hosted the founders of the company along with the Director to demonstrate what abilities my team had for growth.

Evidently, I proved to myself that my dreaming is effective when action is coupled with the imaginative consciousness. Now I am always putting my imaginative mind to work and before you know it I am manifesting my desires.

As human as I am, I began to allow fear, yes "False Evidence Appearing Real" to penetrate my thinking. I wanted to stop being the major force behind growing and going to any of the markets I provided with my MLM experiences. I decided to delegate to my senior team members areas of operation to keep the market moving but to no avail. The first indication of the decline in sales threw me into panic mode and I stayed there for about 3 months. I began to think that I had neglected my family, home and friends in America and should spend some time at home. Unfortunately, things never returned to its blooming state and I was not prepared to invest much more to the development which should have been self-sufficient by then. To me, I did accomplish much success by developing the team from 9 to over 1500 in one country in approximately 2 years.

Since MLM was beginning to look grey on my side of the world, I decided to turn my attention to the development of my personal business. Knowing my strengths in shipping, procurement and logistics, I decided that would be my focus.

I believed that if I put the same energy and focus on my own products or services, the results would be more satisfying than if I was doing it for someone else or another company. With this belief in mind, I decided that if operating my business was the way, I needed to have a vision forward, and so the dreaming continued.

One day on my return from Athens, Greece, as I was walking near my business location and noticed an empty building. I inquired from the store owners and operators next to me but they had no idea of the status of the location. They suggested I call the number of a construction company that was placed on a small yellow ad, posted outside.

I did as I was instructed and the owner contacted me to meet with him at 6:00 p.m. that same day. I did not at the time have any finances air marked for opening this business. All I knew was that I was going to own and operate my own shipping company out of this location. After our brief meeting, I negotiated a lower rent to what he had asked and agreed to meet with his real estate lawyers to move forward.

With little money in my account and no substantial investment funding, I decided to have the dream of everything falling into place with whatever resources I had. Little did I know that sharing my dream with my closest friends and family would materialize the funding needed and support to start and keep the doors of my business opened. I did not tell any of the two persons that finance was an issue but they poured into me and my dream what was needed to start my business.

That night I created the vision/dream that I had the meeting with the lawyers and owner and I convinced them to give the location to me for the price I had asked. I was excited to receive the keys and I could see myself in the office talking to my customers and filling out paper work. I even saw my staff that was not even in existence as yet. In addition, I saw myself writing out the check with the monies needed for rent and security, and handing it over at the time of signing of the contract.

I am so honoured to have the opportunity to dream, dream big, and experiences the rewards of dreaming. So, I am sharing my stories today to inspire others to have your mind set of dreaming big dreams and then avail yourself to the endless opportunities life will present.

# CHAPTER 8

## *My Epiphany*

Essenese Sambury

I was awakened by the sound of a voice and all of a sudden there was pain. I remembered the smell of gunpowder and there was the sound of an explosion. What was that I thought? Was it a memory or a dream? Then I realized that I was in a hospital. Something had happened to me that was causing me pain. Something dreadful had brought me to the hospital. I could not speak and I felt bandages on my face.

Later I came to know that I was shot.... in the face. It slowly came back to me. I had driven into my driveway, on a Sunday afternoon, and then there was a blank.

Friends and family started pouring in to see me. Everybody was sad. That made me sad, at first, but as I lay there on that hospital bed for such long hours at a time, I reflected on life. Things were still in a blur but I was alive.

I needed to get back on my feet. That's my nature, roll with the punches and centre myself. That thought began to consume me, so I became more accepting of my challenged position. Much prayers, much introspection, much thanks for life, later, and a lot of outpouring of love positioned me on the cusp of a new way of life, a rebirth. This was to be my epiphany. I felt it! I came to know it!

I got up one morning, prayed to my God and he revealed to me that I had to rethink my choices, my ways of transacting and my expectations. So I sought fervently to align myself, at least in my mind, with positive vibes, prosperous motives and empowering company. I could not speak, so I wrote. There I was, writing, at a speed, to convey this new aspiration, spelling not being my strongest suit, but I got the messages across. Times like these, one realizes how communication is less about language and more about a sincere transfer of values and sentiment. I was not allowing my plight to daunt my spirits. I insisted that no one was to be sad around me. It was all about resolution. It was about getting better. It was about maintaining balance, in God's name.

After all, I was alive because of Him. I had been shot twice at close range, in the face. One bullet lodged itself in my neck and the other miraculously went through my mouth and out through my neck without destroying my tongue. So talking again was a real possibility, in the future. I had to thank my lucky stars. It was divine intervention, I swear! Granted my jaw was shattered and my teeth were displaced, but all speaking to the probability of successful recovery.

That became my modus operandi - that I will live intentionally - not only to repair my physical self but to elevate my spiritual being. I was always called the come-back-kid, the resilient one, the survivor. This time I felt I had to prove it. I appreciated these accolades but truly I realized that everything happens for a reason. This was my catharsis. I had another chance to fulfil my true destiny. God gave me a second chance,

Before this tragedy, I was a lover of people. Sometimes, more often than not, I put people before me. This naivety led to the negligence of my own priorities so that this wake-up call confirmed that I needed to attend to me a little bit more. I will always be a people person, it's in my DNA. Miliscent, may she rest in peace, passed that on to all her children. We grew up with other people being taken in and being cared for so we all possessed that caring-for-others, beyond the call, spirit.

I simply need to channel my humanitarian spirit in a more uplifting way, not to my detriment or disquiet. The Lord had spoken to me quite lucidly. As I began to speak, garbled though it might have been, I was vehement about my intentions. I told those whom I loved that I love them explicitly. I realized that I could have passed on without my expressing my love for those who matter dearly to me. This made me vigilant and self-aware. The unfortunate circumstance of my life sharpened my sense of humanity

There is indeed a thin line between life and death, one minute you are going about your merry way, the next, you are slumped over a steering wheel, bleeding profusely and out of control. This shock situation was the way to access my therapy. Control is more delusional than we think. God is in control! I have learned that. So my next step is to direct a path to make a more meaningful contribution to those around me and so I proposed to fortify myself with purpose.

I had to fix my face so I charted a way forward with the help of some passionate loving family members and friends. A fundraiser to address the cost of surgery was planned. Some thought I was acting too calculatedly but it became my mission to heal inwardly and outwardly. We are often terrified of taking action particularly when it is to do with our advancement. Our culture has made us apologetic about going after our dreams and goals. In order for me to make a significant shift in psyche, I was to work on the inside with the guidance of the Almighty and purposefully seek to enhance my image, outside. My face had become slightly deformed as a result of the attack. I could barely eat anything, my vision was affected, my hearing was altered and my taste buds were skewed. I had lost a sense of who I was. But I was beginning to find an inner peace which was resonating through everything I did.

Out of the hospital, I had to find myself. I was at odds with my physical reality. It had now hit me how displaced I was as a result of this catastrophe. For indeed it was a catastrophe! For, in spite of the mustering up of mental strength and the acting out of a passionate reason for living and even with my new found faith, it still proved very challenging. Where was the get-up-and-go Essenese. She resided somewhere within me but she just could not actually activate. I was wounded! I had been dealt a grave blow. The only way out of the abyss of my physical incapacity was the nurturing and the nourishing of my spiritual potential. Therein lies the source of will and positive thinking. I had to claim the capacity to regain a sense of self. I had to relinquish myself to my master.

He enlightened me on the possible prospects which could arise out of a turning around the odds. Out of a seemingly negative situation I had to aspire to positive realities. Wherever there were valleys, there would be mountains, I had to rise like a phoenix out of the ashes of despair.

The fundraiser was a hit. A great turnout with fabulous talent was manifested, all to the glory of God. I felt loved. It's really important to feel loved when your life seems overshadowed by fear and insecurity. Ever so often I would ask myself, "Why would anyone want to do me physical harm?" I had to get over that. I also had to deal with the alienation of many for whom I had high regard. This estrangement baffled me and I could not understand the degrees of separation that presented themselves. I cried convulsively. Their reasoning seemed fickle but they had their reasons. I screamed at myself, many a time, "Get over it!"

It happened, the next step is to fix things! My friend in Caracas made the appointments for the surgeries and I was hopeful and optimistic about the future. Probably a little delusional for I thought everything would fix like magic. But that gave me the drive to proceed. However, all the necessary monies were not raised and I wanted to fall into a slump, but I stayed focused on God. Where there is a will, there is a way and God would provide it, I reassured myself

I had been proactive in setting up a little salon so that there was some income, but that was not what I wanted at the time, and it was not the vision for me at that stage of life, post the trauma. So as I readily released to the universe the notion of selling the business a longstanding client, who was interested in taking up an entrepreneurial position, stated that she would buy the salon. What a relief!

If ever before, I denied the existence of God I knew now he is real and he is awesome. Now, I could travel for my surgeries. The Essenese I envisaged was taking shape but only with the help of Jesus.

This part of my journey, I celebrate openly and I give praise wholeheartedly. My faith had deepened. I remained true as possible to the teachings of the Holy Book and I worshipped every chance I got with congregations of sisters and brothers. This is a testimony because of a revelation. I was brought back to the Father as a result of a great misfortune. Now, I no longer see the stress as an unnecessary hardship, I see it as a necessary evil.

Some of us may have to traverse very difficult routes to access the truth. I certainly did but I feel all the better for having done so. After marriage, yes, I got married, I settled in the Bahamas, where I remain committed to my God. I use my experiences as lessons to share with others. The most important thing about life is giving and sharing joy. You better believe it. My new work family commemorated my birthday with such simplicity and honesty and I was so overjoyed. I do not miss the fanfare of doing things on a larger scale. The simpler things in life bring me great satisfaction and indeed, serving my God. There is a contentment in a new beginning I had to let go and let God do. Now I can do. It is so empowering without the clutter of otherworldly expectations. I see myself growing and becoming more fulfilled. I have certainly changed the way I look at things and I have seen that the things I look at have changed.

## *A little about Dr. Sonia Noel*

Dr Sonia Noel is a passionate and industrious creative artist and bestselling author with a fresh New World perspective on style and life. Sonia Noel is celebrating over 20 years in the fashion industry. It took a combination of navigational skills to out-manoeuvre hurdles and a resilience to literally row her own boat when the waters got rough. Small town girl with a big dream who believed it was possible. She celebrates her Amerindian roots, but she is no "woman of straw" yet she utilized this indigenous South American creativity and cosmopolitan

## *A little about Dr. Sonia Noel*

Caribbean flair, to craft a unique fashion aesthetic that is identifiably, the Sonia Noel brand.

Her determined spirit pushes her to drive creative industry enterprise forward and she has become an exemplar and mentor to young creatives, not only in Guyana, but throughout the region. She has been presented with many awards locally, regionally and even internationally, for entrepreneurship, philanthropy, cultural ambassadorial services , advancing creative enterprise, promoting competitive- worthy fashion design and youth empowerment. Her designs can be worn from the beach to the ballroom.Well known names who wore her designs are Maxi Priest, Miss Universe Leila Lopez and Michelle Williams former Destiny's Child member.

Originating from a hamlet, up the Essequibo, far removed from the capital, where her dreams of becoming a fashion designer might have appeared far-fetched and illusory, she pioneered, persevered and eventually positioned her brand as a sought-after regional trendsetter, with international

## *A little about Dr. Sonia Noel*

appeal. From her early collections, in Georgetown, relying on her geographic, architectural and Afro-Amerindian references, she has evolved into the quintessential Guyanese designer, influencing, impactfully, the Caribbean aesthetic, having shown in the major capitals of the region, she has gone on to the metropolises of the world, where there is an active Diaspora influence - London, Los Angeles, Atlanta, Washington, Boston, Texas, New Jersey, Miami, Spain, China, India New York, Toronto, Montreal. Sonia Noel is a true "woman of substance"!

Sonia Noel is the founder of Guyana Fashion Week, The Women's Association for Sustainable Development, The Women in Business Expo, Guyana Model Search, Designers Portfolio and the Sonia Noel Foundation for Creative Arts.

Her work was featured in numerous publications in the Caribbean and around the world. Ms Noel is a columnist in the Guyana Sunday Chronicle News Papers -Beyond the Runway. She is also a John Maxwell Speaker, Coach and Trainer.

# LIVING WITH INTENTION
## Motivational Tour

I have launched my first book **LIVING WITH INTENTION - Commit, Contribute, Celebrate on** November 24th, 2018. The LIVING WITH INTENTION Motivational Tour and online program was launched as a result of this bestselling book on Amazon.

**LIVING WITH INTENTION Motivational** Tour and Online program will offer you a glimpse into that world that makes every day a masterpiece, even with life's challenges.

**LIVING WITH INTENTION** will take you to the core of survival, to the importance of how to love and why you should celebrate. You will be inspired to want to do because in the doing you become.

**LIVING WITH INTENTION** will motivate those who are still struggling to be the best version of themselves.

If you are interested in contributing to the tour or joining the online program, email
livingwithintention11@gmail.com
or call +592 684 8129.

# ICON**MEDIA**
P H O T O G R A P H Y

AT 'IM' PHOTOGRAPHY WE UNITE
ART AND PHOTOGRAPHY
TO CAPTURE AND PRESERVE
YOUR MOST VALUABLE MOMENTS.

FASHION
WEDDING
FAMILY
EVENT
CORPORATE

## MAKE YOUR BOOKINGS

email:
askme@iconmedia.gy

mobile:
658 3803

# Connections
## TRAVEL SERVICE

☑ **Local Tours**

☑ **Local Interior Flights**

☑ **Best International Fares**

☎ 592-227-2810, 592-227-2832, 592-225-0380

🖷 592-227-2999

✉ connections@connectionsgy.com

🌐 connectionsgy.com

📍 6 Avenue of the Republic, Georgetown, Guyana, South America.

# Dr. SONIA E. NOEL D.H.L
### Designer, Producer, Philanthropist, Life Coach

mobile: +592 684 8129
email: soniaenoel@gmail.com

office : +592 226 6554
web: www.sonianoel.com

Made in the USA
Columbia, SC
08 March 2021